First printing

For my beautiful daughters:

Brooklyn MacKenzie
Arianna Rae

My little beams of lights who guide me through the dark
whenever I lose my way.

Keep that light inside your heart
....*always*

PART I

Between Two Worlds

We live our lives
between two worlds;
sometimes,
existing only
as

a memory,
a fleeting thought,
a distant taste
in the back
of the mouth.

A reminder that
although truth may
penetrate the aphotic
cloak of secrecy
in short,

the distant alcoves
of our mind,
of our body,
of our essence
remain secure.

Crescendo builds;
anti-climactic
in its first solo
performance,
yet still

impressive in its
own odd way.
Persistence
holds its own
to prove

that we're still here.
Yet, lacking
belief and
faith and
trust.

Mere ghosts, we long
to be accepted,
to be loved,
to be freed
from

this trite purgatory.
The tragedy being
that we will never
be able to
escape.

Refusal to acquiesce
our souls in entirety;
forever doomed
to exist between
two worlds.

El Beso de la Muerte (Kiss of Death)

Winged suitor adorned in
marble doth grant thy new
lover an embrace of stone.
Eternal caress with lips as
cold as dark earth beckon.

This ossein stroke, a touch
I crave even as repugnance
settles into my cursed soul.
Plucked at instant of ripest
fruition by ethereal prince.

A rose be placed in seeking
hands with tender grace; a
bouquet of thorns to soothe,
as widows grieve lucid tears
to be washed away as blood.

Oh sweet death, I beseech
thee, welcome me in your
decaying arms, unyielding.
This imploration a mystery
to my own pillaged youth.

Bring me to my knees in all
magnificence and carry me
to my everlasting crypt, oh
stunning creature of Hades.
A morbid wonder to behold.

Taste on sapid tongue, my
final breath; unsanctified
awakening of immortality.
One last kiss on waxen skin
before vacant eyes do sleep.

A Perfect Place to Die

Sentinel of stone, keep morbid
watch; a silent contemplation
as death swallows eager souls.
For these are the forsaken ones
who surrender themselves to
drown alone in the Sea of Trees.

Insatiable forest shrouded in
despair demands atonement,
though not through coercion.
Each new acquisition, a prize
bestowed without provocation;
thus, no need for repentance.

Lush foliage murmurs in faint
whispers of protest, in brief,
before yielding in resignation.
Bony fingers guide the way to
paths as stony as the hearts that
seek solitude; a retreat for the lost.

Ancient Ubasate, a fitting demise
among branches withered gray?
Justification perhaps, for those
remaining to mourn youth bygone.
Vehement in its apathetic nature,
an abandonment of convenience

Once choice be made, in all accord,
the spirits nod approval, detached
yet locked in eternal connection.
Centuries of haunted screams of
the damned be muted only by the
resounding quietude of Aokigahara.

Ignis Fatuus

Hope
Love
Dreams..

Incandescent delusions
dancing at the precipice
of docile, pliable minds.
Just a misleading mirage
easily blinded by naivety;
swiftly aborted by reality.

Logic
Insight
Rationale..

Impeded by intangible
twine so tightly trussed.
Bonds securely constrict;
A suitable solution to a
futile and pointless stab
at resistance; uncertain.

Integrity
Reason
Purpose..

Sequestered behind an
opaque yet impenetrable
veil of subterfuge; this
is a sad play of pretence.
Persevering appears to be
impractical; asinine really.

Hollow
Melancholy
Insignificant..

A slow progression of
lamentation lacking any
emotion, but harbouring
just enough adequacy to
suppress the precariously
mounting pressure inside.

Forlorn
Disconsolate
Resigned..

Desolate, barren soul.
The future pimps out
a blank page to a frigid
paramour; an inkless pen.
Aptly narrated by silence,
by solitude; the tale ends.

Dejected
Bereft
Soulless..

Non Compos Mentis

Alabaster skin glows
under the moon's gaze;
the only witness to the
night's grisly antics.
The secrets stored in
craters deep and dark.

And so, the shadows
born in dusk soften
the harsh brutality
of what he has done.
The raving voices fall
silent, briefly buried.

Her blood, a viscous
pool of ebony sits mute,
like a lazy afterthought;
stagnant and forgotten.
The callous earth laps it
up, deliriously inebriated.

The primal urge to take
a life, for now, contained.
In time, the rage will
crest again, and only
the tangy taste of blood
can quench the thirst.

The night tells no tales
and reveals no clues he
deems to be discreet.
Preferring to bask in the
glory of exquisite deaths
as if they were his own.

It's Not the Destination

My journey ends as
it began, in darkness
and blind confusion.
And all that dwells
in between consists
of a corrupted exhibit
of fractured images.
Light; thin, unsteady
fragments penetrate
nebulous wafers of
obscurity, casting
back sly glances with
such haunting clarity.
If only snippets of
time could be paused
at will and displayed
in pensive nostalgia
rather than packed
into some forgotten
chamber of ashes.
But, this adventure
isn't meant to remain
stationary or eternal.
It is a fleeting spark
in the universe that
can only be captured
briefly and cherished
for whatever minute
span of time has been
befittingly granted
How we utilize this
precious gift that has
been bestowed upon
us is a personal choice.
It's quite a pity that
this realization fails
to penetrate our smug
arrogance until the
flame has died down
to a tendril of smoke;
fading to nothingness.

What Time Can Tell

What doesn't kill me
better fucking run.
I'm not the same
timid girl that you
knew me to be so
long ago; just an
amicable warning.
I am still me, but
A more enhanced
version, with a few
minor adjustments.
My metamorphosis,
agony indescribable
in any language, was
worth every wound
and every lasting scar.
Isolated in a cocoon,
protected from both
good and evil, I was
fortunate enough to
observe the world
as it really is; a cold
and unforgiving hell.
But it is a hell of our
own personal design.
Abound with irony;
the way these murky
waters of jealousy
and animosity can
clear the perception.
Undaunted by my
disclosure, you'll
stubbornly persist.
So, I'll bide my
time and you can
squander yours.

Words of Wisdom

After dark, I see the
light that marks the
way to exoneration.
Refreshing how the
cloak of dusk allows
bonds of humanity
to be so easily shed.
We move from one
skin to another in
hopes that, by some
chance, we will find
our impeccable fit.
This performance,
acted out in a less
than stellar manner,
surprisingly, isn't
eagerly offered up
as fodder to critics.
Instead, it is viewed
as entertainment;
tolerated as a most
welcome diversion
from the bullshit
we would rather
not focus on when
handed a few free
moments of time.
I would prefer not to
prolong my stay in
such dismal quarters.

A wise (?) friend
once served up a
rather refreshing
tidbit of advice on
which to dine upon:

"Stay drunk, my
friend and listen
to the voices."

I believe I will.

Woe is You

What then, if thy be wronged,
shall it be called on this day?
A travesty? A sin? A prank?
Oh, the injustice protesting to
nonchalant ears in sour tones.
Such tactics fail to move me,
so deem my heart to be a bed
of stone; a notion of triviality.
Past conduct speaks volumes
of reflection to secure insight.

Forever suffering, the helpless
victim; a tragic tale you weave.
Whoring out flagrant emotions
with delusive tact, you fumble
for apologies spoken only out
of obligation, a necessary duty.
A role worthy of accolades and
awards; quite a dramatic scene.
What bounty do you gain from
this ornate exhibition? Pray tell.

Is boredom that distasteful of
a comrade that you must stray?
Or is it amusement that serves
to tweak your fancy thus so?
Whichever die you opt to roll,
the numbers cannot be fixed to
your favour; the house always
reaps the winnings silly bitch.
Usually so meticulous in your
preparation, you disappoint me.

Listen to the Dead

Granite stones, scrubbed
smooth by saddened rains.
Words ineligible, speak
of lost lives adrift in time.
Awakened by dark's loyal
caress, the dead appear to
tell their tales, if you care
to entertain their thoughts.

Beneath the comfort of the
cold, hard ground, they rest.
Forgotten by passing years,
pain lessens with time, for
the living, so I've been told.
No one considers the dead
as they wither to dust and
wash away in convenience.

In truth, perceived as mere
vessels, and nothing more,
they search for an attentive
audience in which to dispute
their case. Quite a compelling
argument they present, by
witness of night's fleeting
shadows; it has commenced.

The moon retains the
right to turn its head;
out of fear or apathy,
the rationale, a mystery.
The dead traverse the
bridge between their
world and ours in search
of unobtainable answers.

My spirit is disheartened.
I clutch at hope that when
my soul disembarks this
world, I will have finally
found the resolution I seek.
Roaming the hereafter with
with no purpose is more
terrifying than death itself,

HAIKUS

Sakura

Blushing spring blossoms
Intoxicating fragrance
Japanese delight

Kaleidoscope

Autumn hues ablaze
Composing abstract canvas
Summer's final dance

Sahara's Sweetheart

Desert sentinel
Thriving in barren wastelands
Hope amid bleakness

Ode to Zoe

A butterfly's charm
Vibrant petals reach heaven
Glorious tributes

Sea of Green

Emerald ocean
Luscious carpet underfoot
Summer's sweet essence

Accalia

Swift ghost of the night
Bare your soul to the full moon
Your lament be heard

Ascending to Heaven

Majestic in death
Sharp talons at the ready
Freedom be my love

Misabe Mukwa

Great lumbering beast
Ruler of the dark forest
Hot breath chills the spine

White Death

Ravenous hunter
Danger disguised by beauty
Strikes without warning

Siren of the Seas

Haunting symphony
Transcending the vast oceans
A humpback's sweet song

Arachnophobia

Dew glistens on silk
Beautiful spun masterpiece
Deadly seduction

Queen of the Jungle

Sleek tawny huntress
Amber eyes lock in on prey
Swift bite to the throat

Snake Eyes

Slithering serpent
Stalking rodents with forked tongue
Graceful in the grass

Bearded Dragon

Camouflaged dragon
Feasting on crunchy crickets
Basking in the sun

Squirrels

Beady little eyes
Chattering in annoyance
Scrambling up branches

Crystalline

Virgin tapestry
Encrusted with gleaming gems
The earth can now sleep

On Cloud Nine

Keepers of the skies
Billowy white shape shifters
Obscuring the sun

Purification

Teardrops of the Gods
Tiny morsels of heaven
Quenching arid souls

Elysian Fields

Electric fingers
Split open darkening skies
Heaven's wrath unleashed

Go With the Floe

Majestic giant
Forever frozen in time
What secrets below?

Puddles

Refreshing droplets
Descending from the heavens
Creating ripples

White Horses

Absconding ocean
Reappears with a vengeance
To swallow its meal

Get the Hell Out of Kansas

Spiral of darkness
Tumultuous pirouette
Pure devastation

Fire in the Sky

Celestial fire
Plummet from heavenly perch
The night sky's passion

Rainbow

From tempest is born
Connecting heaven and earth
Perfection exists

Terra Firma

Sustainer of life
From whence all creatures exist
We return to dust

Umiko

Sparkling bed of blue
What mysteries to behold
Beneath her facade

In a Blaze of Glory

On glowing embers
Mesmerizing colours sway
To music unheard

Blow Me

Feather light caress
Chaotic Choreographs
By unseen fingers

PART II

Sanctimonious Duplicity

The flames, they exonerate
me from my self-inflicted
verdict and incarceration.
I care not for convictions
of others; they are moot,
suspect and disputable.
The weight of external
influences is a burden we
must choose to discard.
Until we do, the colours
remain dull and boring;
absolutely unremarkable.
Inhibitions; the invisible
restraints of uncertainty
and warped perceptions
cause us to waver, falter.
Escape can be achieved if
we hold confidence in our
ability to rise above faults.
But acceptance does not
carry a guarantee nor a
certificate of authenticity.
Words are only hollow
echoes of false bravery.
It is with deep remorse
that I admit I'm too weak
to heed my own advice.

A Paradox Indeed

A tale be told of
two forks in a road,
each leading to a
fate of some worth.

Oh reason, be mute;
'tis my call to make.
Which path be it -
blessing or curse?

Uttered so sweet,
lies lighten the soul;
while truth votes on
which havoc to wreak.

A voice do you hear?
Well, pay it no heed.
Of what myth in your
heart can it speak?

My, they are pretty,
I'm sure you'll agree,
the slick words of a
silver-tipped tongue.

Conveniently blind,
no scruples to bear,
faith silences trust
for....pure....fun.

Illusions of Immortality

To challenge Destiny
Is to embark on a futile
quest, for She creates
the rules as the game
progresses, tweaking
them at a mere whim.
Still, you embrace the
notion that you have
the ability to alter the
course of your fate by
spinning the wheel.
This juvenescent itch
you harbour; it only
serves to mock the
powers that be, who
in essence, control
full jurisdiction of
your accursed soul.
The blame you cast
in full is your own
and you must tend
to it as so instructed.
If you just accept the
fact that your legend,
as it were, has been
drafted long ago and
cannot be edited at
your personal desire.
If you could truly
comprehend this
axiom, then perhaps
Destiny will be a
little more lenient
with your pathetic,
remorseless soul.

Trails of Temptation

Lead me where the path recedes,
by stagnant waters, dark and deep.
You're not held to any obligation,
by the way, to follow me through
the storm; I won't ask this of you.

Ambiguous mediums escort me
to venues they assume I belong
and knowing the sketchy images
that manifest in my warped mind,
their guesses are perfectly accurate.

Why must the conscience always
prove to be such a braggart and a
bore? Would it be so scandalous
to turn a blind eye, just this once,
to my blasphemous frivolities?

Temptations close in with foliage
bewitching, yet malignant in its
potential. Asphyxiation seems a
most welcome demise; almost
euphoric in its warm embrace.

If curiosity plays in your favour,
feel free to join me in my quest.
I offer you a fair warning, if my
discretions are not to your taste,
it was your decision to follow me.

In Search Of....

Her name, a whisper in
the passing winds, spoken
with hushed uneasiness.
Dark and deep, secrets
held in shame keep their
silence; forced in death.

What atrocities entombed
beneath unforgiving dirt
do paralyze the sanity?
Tragedy serves to wrench
the heart in two, a rend to
which no antidote exists.

Arthritic branches speak
of unjust tales, only when
prodded by urgent gusts.
Mysteries spilled through
falling leaves, sacrificed
beneath mourning feet.

Echoes murmured in the
falling rains weep laments
of restitution withheld.
A curse betrothed upon
her soul, and so deserved,
yet only death shall know.

Void of remorse for sins
committed, blame is cast
onto passers of judgment.
A deed that screams of
aberrant hypocrisy, yet
holds validity in madness.

In search of disclosure
she wanders; not fully
considering the questions.
In search of absolution,
she roams; oblivious to
the futility of her quest.

Falling Star

A falling star, letting go
of heaven holds faith that
earth will reward her with
an even more valuable prize.

So, I placed trust in myself.
Drifting through space, no
clear destination in mind,
I found my way to you.

A place of rest, or so I
thought; sweet solitude.
Much needed sanctuary
built exclusively for me.

A touching gesture; love.
How was I to know that
felicity flings open the
doors, inviting heartache?

A strategic move; I applaud you.

No war is strictly won by
the victor's tactics alone.
To be fair, some accolades
must be granted to the loser.

When emotion trumps reason;
this is the instant when defeat
sets in – defeat or surrender.
Either way, you're fucked.

Disheartened, the falling star
returns to orbit, chagrined
that she is unable to secure
her original place in the skies.

A supernova, flaring bright
at the moment just before
implosion; self destruction.
Beauty matched by none.

All that remains is a black hole.

A Cold Dish

I can understand how
agonizing the pain is
at the moment; it burns.
A part of you has been
forever altered and this
ruthless act of betrayal
must be justly avenged.
Be patient my friend.
Allow the fire to run
its course and know that
although the embers are
no longer visible, they
still remain, smouldering
beneath white hot ashes.
It takes only a tiny puff
of wind to send them
raging again, stronger.
Ah, the iciness that grips
your heart; feel it melting.
It's like your soul is rising
from the dead, like being
reborn, don't you agree?
You may not be rewarded
with the chance to bear
witness, but the time will
come when all arrears are
paid, when the ticket is
punched for the last time.
This will be your restitution.
Your meal, once finally
served, will be the tastiest
feast you've ever dined upon.
Hold faith in this; I do.

You're Breaking My Heart

You're breaking my heart.
These pitiful tales of woe
that weep from your lips.
You do realize I can see
through the dirty gauze
so carelessly wrapped in
a cheap effort to dull the
impact of your deception.

Blinded by pure arrogance,
you perform so brilliantly.
I'll play your game, if only
to entertain my curiosity.
Besides, I'd like to see how
far your pompous egotism
will transport you before
the layers start to unravel.

How sweet the thought is;
your credibility tarnished,
your aspirations crushed,
your will broken; defunct.
Satisfaction, a freeloading
parasite that nestles into
the rationale, replacing it
with numbing vengeance.

I do not fear the wrath of
Karma for these ill wishes
I harbour against you; Why?
Its no different than the way
the moon contemplates the
sun's last dying breath as it
sinks deep into the horizon.
My soul rests in tranquility.

This sequence, this endless
cycle, it's no mystery as to
the methodical reasoning.
'Tis just the natural scheme
of the world and I, a simple
bystander, patiently wait,
ensuring that all the pieces
fall as they are intended.

Ties that Bind

The ties that bind are
easily torn and once
they're upon the mend,
if you peer real close
to where they join, you
will always see the ends.

For no matter how you
try to cleanse your soul,
it can never become pure.
The heart will be forever
marred from the agony
that you've endured.

Words can stab so hard,
so deep; and they can
never be taken back.
Each one a sharp dagger,
soaked in salty tears; a
fierce and cruel attack.

Life is not a comfy
ride. It is fraught
with pain and grief.
The path we tread
can lead to hell. Our
time on earth is brief.

Knowing this, what will
you do? Will you turn
your head and snub?
Or, will you yield,
and admit your faults?
Ahh, now, there's the rub.

Reality Check

Life,

Nothing more than
mundane
repetitive
oscillations
arduously blending
into another then another
and yet another.

Knowledge gained;
an epiphany,
if you will,
that all you have
yearned for
has dissipated.

That turn you
ignored back there?
Perhaps,
you should have
chosen it instead of
blindly staggering
down the
easier trail.

You must understand
the truth
about hindsight.
If we all possessed
such wisdom, then
none would harbour
regrets,
nor remorse,
nor second thoughts.

Instead, we cling to
the notion that,
at some point,
we will arrive
at the place we
have always imagined
Eden to be.

Only,
Eden isn't exactly
what was found.
Crude awakening isn't it?
To find so many years
have sped along
and you are nowhere close
to being the person
so carefully planned in
your carefree days
of naivety and youth.

Reality check my friend:
Life goes on with or without
a carefully planned itinerary,
and even if you have one,
well,
it really makes no
difference anyway.

Life
makes the
final call.

Shitty isn't it?

EROTIC
(Explicit Content)

A Death Worth Living

The gates of paradise,
they entice me with
their alluring scent.
Soft petals part with
the gentlest nudge.
Glistening diamonds
of nectareous dew,
how delicious they
taste; dancing with
fervour on my seeking
tongue, and greedily
I drink, as if enjoying
my last meal on this
sultry earth. Her breath
quickens as I continue
to feast on forbidden
fruit to which only a
chosen few have been
granted entry. This
invitation, an honour
to behold in such
exclusivity. I dare not
squander this amorous
gift, choosing instead
to offer a bequest of
my own, in fairness.
My just reward, in
truth, is rousing the
feral beast that lay
dormant for so long.
To hear it roar in pure
ecstasy and feel its
taut mouth clench my
entire being until we
both collapse is truly
A death worth living.

A Woman Scorned

I savour the tongue of
the lash as it strokes
my supple, ivory skin.
Even as I cry out from
the pain, I can feel the
cravings stirring from
deep within my being.
My back, it arches in
anticipation of your
thrusts, just as hard and
brutal as the whip before.
Grab my ass, I beseech,
as if you actually have a
choice in the matter at all.
For it is I who hold the
controls of every action,
every motion, and every
whisper that transpires
between our hot, writhing
bodies. The frantic rhythm
increases and I take all that
I desire with no regrets, no
pause, no second thoughts.
With one last lick of my
lips, I gather up my dress,
my torn panties and walk
out the door, refusing to
cast a final glance back.

I hope she can smell my
lingering scent on your
body and see the betrayal
that emanates from your
eyes when she returns.
Transgressions and their
consequences should be
thoroughly researched
before plunging ahead;
I'm sure you agree.

Behind Closed Doors

Concealed from eyes
both prying and full
of judgement, they
shed sinful inhibitions
that they themselves
perceive as deplorable
and quite shameful.
Oh my, what would
The chaste and pure
of heart think if only
they knew? The games
played behind closed
doors, how they quicken
the pulse and awaken
emotions inside that lay
long forgotten. Here, in
hushed secrecy all may
bare their soul to those
who care to sample a
delicacy few others
have the courage or
passion to exhibit. Here,
fantasy is the only rule;
you can be anyone, do
anything; act out any
corrupt role the wicked
mood of the moment
can devise in pleasure.
I challenge your denial
to partake in jovialities
of such naughty nature.

The knowing glimmer
in your eyes contradicts
your feeble objections.
Betrayed by your own
body, you will obey me.
For behind closed doors,
no one will breathe a word.

Dirty Bitch

I'll be your trash,
I'll be your treasure,
I'll be whatever
you want me to be.
A proper young lass?
A promiscuous whore?
A naughty schoolgirl?
I'll play out your dream.

Go on; punish my flesh
in sick, twisted ways
Force me down to
my hands and my knees.
Chain me and whip me
'til I beg you to stop.
Show no mercy and
heed not my pleas.

I want to be dirty
I want to be yours.
Confess to me your
most wicked desires.
Every sick fantasy
that enters your mind
will only help stoke
my pussy's hot fire.

With no hesitation
I'll allow you to taste
the Promised Land
that waits deep within.
Tease me; please me,
'til I scream with delight
The way you fuck me,
it must be a sin.

I care not for the values
nor opinions of those
who think it's immoral
to travel down south.
Perhaps if they try it,
just once, they'll agree;
you can have fun with
a cock in your mouth.

Give me your fingers.
Yes, put them right there.
Can you feel I'm soaked
from your caress?
I want you inside me;
to fuck me once more.
Please, just take me.
I'll always say yes.

Do You Like to Watch?

Do you like to watch?

...as I brush my soft hair
with such slow, deliberate
strokes, sliding down from
root to shaft, root to shaft.
So soft against my hand.

Do you like to watch?

...as I slip my silky robe
off my shoulder, bare skin
awash in moonlight's gaze.
It falls, a glistening puddle
at my feet; I'm in shadows.

Do you like to watch?

...as I display myself on
sheets of satin; heaven
upon my burning skin,
The contrast heightens
my unfulfilled needs.

Do you like to watch?

...as I gently squeeze my
supple breasts and pinch
the nipples; they are hard
and swollen. Delicious
shivers invade my body.

Do you like to watch?

...as I slide one, then two
fingers inside my aching
wetness; deeper I plunge,
increasing speed until I
break into pulsing spasms.

Do you like to watch?

...as I lick my own sweet
juices off my wet finger.
With enticing slowness, I
suck at each one, knowing
full well that you see all.

Would you like to join me?

Incubus

Incubus, I summon
thee, no, I command
thee; come forward.
Bring me to release
from this primal lust
and gnawing urgency
that devours me in full.
Unleash unrestrained
virility; oh you great
beast of all desires
carnal and lecherous.
Take me, for tonight
I am your whore to
use in any way you
so please. In brazen
and shameless wanton,
I eagerly offer myself
to your whims. The
ecstasy; an intense
hunger that consumes
sanity and lucidity.
Promise me instant
sexual gratification
and in return, I will
grant you the wish
to defile me in ways
so unspeakable and
vile to those who view
themselves to be both
virtuous and void of
immortality. How rich!

As if such a soul exists!
Spent, I crave solitude.
So, away with you and
your deliciously wicked
ways. Back to my filthy
dreams you can morph,
to await my next invitation.

La Petite Mort

Reason be doused
by sweet nectar.
Oh, the taste on
toxic tongue be
rousing to the
verge of death;
but not beyond.

Not yet....

Torture, blessed
torture, be thy
guide, I beg of
you; offer me
nothing more
than swift
and complete

....release.

Through fevered
flesh, expel thy
lust, thy carnal
sins; unquenched.
Exquisite pain,
embrace my soul.
Each little death

pure....bliss.

Thy inhibition
take leave, and
virtue depart.
Chastity, be
held at bay.
Reborn in haste,
I long to die

..once more..

Make Me Clean

I'm a dirty girl, yes it's true.
I can't deny how I want you.
Pull me close, I crave a kiss.
Pale blue eyes, I can't resist.
Bulging, longing to be free.
That you can entrust to me.

Rip your shirt, lick your chest,
I knew you'd offer no protest.
Standing nude, I hold the power.
Will you join me in the shower?
Two bodies join in wicked lust,
ready for your first hard thrust.

Roaming hands, searching lips,
expert fingers, grinding hips.
Water sluices down my skin,
I'm hot and wet, so slide it in.
Pound me; fuck me 'til I scream,
fill my pussy with your cream.

I'm your slave, be my master,
fuck me harder, fuck me faster.
Balls banging against my ass.
I never said I had much class.
Grab my breasts and go in deep.
At the edge, I take that leap.

Milky legs 'round your waist,
all thoughts of purity erased.
In ecstasy, I gouge my nails,
leave behind crimson trails.
Bend me over on all fours.
Shamelessly I beg for more.

Shivers race inside my being.
Carnal acts can be so freeing.
Cum runs thick down my thigh.
Vibrations slow, I give a sigh.
Once sanity and breath regain,
I grab your cock – let's go again!

Making the Grade

Plaid and pleats of red and green,
hair up in braids, blue eyes serene.

Legs crossed in chaste, virtue pure.
Only the surface appears demure.

A promise of pleasure lies between.
You'd never guess her age; sixteen.

Licking lips with thoughts impure;
despite her age, she's quite mature.

Lock the door and pull the blinds.
Alone in lust, you're both confined.

Fuck me now, she begs you, please,
as tongue and mouth begin to tease.

Against your desk, her back inclined,
she'll be a lady and whore combined.

Fingers grab your cock and squeeze;
and stroking hard, sinks to her knees.

Expert tongue swirls slowly around.
Writhing in bliss, you utter no sound.

This aching hunger won't be denied;
tear off her panties, thrust deep inside.

Then bend her over, her ass you pound.
In pure ecstasy you both nearly drown.

Pussy so wet, as your bodies collide,
rubbing her clit, you open her wide.

Pleasure beyond any desire you wish.
Any trace of guilt you quickly dismiss.

So hard and rough, she loves your abuses,
but hopes this tryst left no lasting bruises.

The fire is fed, as it's slowly diminished,
you collapse on top, explode and finish.

She smoothes her skirt, wipes off the juices.
She's earned that A; you have no excuses.

PART III

Chameleon

The sunset always seems prettiest
at the very second before it dies;
as most hopes, dreams and desires
in this fucked up world seem to be.

Stubbornly, we cling to promises,
placing belief in silly calumniations.
How amusing failure's bitter taste
seems as it lingers on the palate.

As the fickle whore's colours fade,
she offers to the night, the saddened
souls of the pathetic and naive mortals
she has collected throughout the day.

What perverse and wicked games
they play as darkness claims the world
as his for a time, and we can only ponder
with fear and dread what lies in wait.

Finally, as dawn peeks her head o'er
the distant horizon, humanities useless
ways become a bore and he spits the
precious cargo back where it belongs.

Salvageable? To some, perhaps.
And others? Well, they go on as
usual, blissfully unaware that their
purpose has been forever changed.

Manifestations of Normality

In the delta of cognition,
visions groan; in truth,
breeding murky thoughts
in the archives of the mind.
How easy to lose the way
through catacombs and
corridors less travelled.
Only a fool would boast
to know the road to sanity
or beyond and in haste
plunge on, regardless of
consequence or resolution.
A paradise for the weak
ripe with pure ignorance;
eager to behold the marvel
emerging from blank canvas.
Realization, if so attained,
is stamped with a bounty
often repaid over time, in
instalments; on a contract
sealed by misled impulse.
Abstract guise painted by
skilled strokes cover the
blemishes; hide the stains.
Unquestionably, not to be
denied, delusion oozes
through the spectrum,
refracted into a multitude
of personas; a perfect
menagerie to be abused.
No matter how beautified,
such pretence fails to infinitely
conceal what lurks beneath.
Such is the way of madness.

Ravenous

My dear, could I
trouble you for a
piece of your soul?
Mine seems to be
corrupt as of late.
It will be returned,
you needn't fear.
Although I can't,
in good faith, offer
up the promise that
its eminence will
remain unscathed.
Untouched by sin
you proclaim to be,
but, c'mon, we're
both aware of what
you have done; why
must you protest?
You self-righteous
bitch, how dare you
entertain the notion
you hold supremacy
over me, when your
own pathetic life is
erratically spiralling
down the precipice.
You boldly balance
between the darkness
and the light; a game
of chance even you
cannot manipulate.

You will slip, you will
stumble and you will
plummet to whichever
side hungers the most.
Feed the beast well
my dear, feed it well.

Self Assessment

The measure of a man's true worth
lies not in material gains,
but rather how he lives his life
and what legacy remains.

For once our souls do tend to pass
from this earthly world beyond,
judgment lies not within our grade
but in how our hearts respond.

So tell me friend, if so inclined
if your journey came to a close,
would your imprint be remembered?
I guess only you can truly know.

If you had but one single wish
to steer you through your life,
would you opt for wealth beyond your dreams,
or would you forever banish strife?

Would selfish thoughts consume your mind
and fill your home with trends?
Or would common eyes with less to bear
melt your heart and call you friend?

The rights and wrongs of all our deeds
are decisions we each must choose.
For in the end there is no one else
who decides if we win or lose.

Until We Meet Again

Your hand I felt upon my cheek
when I knelt beside your grave.
I'm sure you fully comprehend
the peace that this touch gave.

Others, well they will insist it
was the wind tousling my hair.
Only you and I can truly know
the unique bond we still share.

I feel you in the sun's embrace
and in spring's soothing rains.
They serve to melt the icy grief
and to cleanse away my stains.

As I walk along this path alone,
I know you always walk beside.
My home and bed ring empty,
but in my heart you still reside.

Memories fade like tattered silk,
your loving voice I long to hear.
I miss the mornings I'd wake up
with you whispering in my ear.

The silence echoes everywhere;
it nearly drives me to the brink.
You help to calm my saddened
soul, allowing me time to think.

Times we shared, both good
and bad, bring a smile to my lips.
The way you used to look at me
with your hands upon your hips.

The smile falls as I read the words
etched forever on granite stone.
Our time together on this earth
was the greatest I've ever known.

A day will come when its my time,
and I'll get to see your face again.
No purpose left, I'll wander here,
my spirit half dead inside til then.

Walk a Mile

My shoes, they won't fit you.
Go on, give them a try.
Walk as far as you want to.
Are they comfy? Don't lie!

Don't presume that you know
all that exemplifies me.
A perfect deception
is life, can't you see?

A plight so complex
that no man can explain.
You seek all the answers
you will never obtain.

So gather your stones up.
Throw as much as you choose.
Will they hurt me? You bet!
But it's not me who will lose.

So perfect and flawless
does a diamond appear.
Look closer at the image
that you see in the mirror.

The cracks and the fissures
though minute, still remain.
The words and the gestures
on my heart leave a stain.

I guess I should thank you
for the strength I have found.
Although to achieve that
my self-worth has been bound.

Cruel Intentions

Cruelty was never my intention
but temptation presents quite a
compelling argument in favour.
Entwining fact with fiction, its
amusing, your unwavering trust
that decisions are made of your
own accord. Unconvinced, you
have the audacity to question
my bluntness; are you that daft?

What punishment then is fitting
for the crime? If validation is not
forthcoming, I shall walk away
unscathed with no guilt to bear.
I cannot be held accountable if
you were willing; your resolve
is of absolutely no consequence.
Take responsibility for the hand
you play, don't use the pity card.

Promises were designed to be
prescriptions for fools, a means
to mask pain and soothe sorrow.
A temporary fix, yet one we are
addicted to. We crave dependency.
And what of love? It is our bane,
The El Dorado we hopelessly hunt
for but will never find. We settle,
satisfied with a pretty imitation.

Enticing are the images invoked
by deviating thoughts of random.
They float unhindered by regret,
unrestrained by stale perception.
This malicious toxicity, to me, is
confounding; a proclamation that
makes it all the more inebriating.
Seeds of malice fed by tears of
betrayal breed supreme corruption.

The ability to manipulate hearts
and mould minds is a powerful
incentive, one that can obliterate
prudence, wisdom, and acumen.
With consequences overlooked,
freedom to express control reigns.
Infinite scenarios play out and I
reach an epiphany so enthralling;
my actions are laced with cruelty.

On Stanger Tides

As mourning eyes set sail on tides
of septic shores, shallow as the soul,
so does betrayal lap at sands of hope.
Shall we say sorrow's triumph over
love lies not in the conquest but in
devastation flayed open in its wake?
Behold, a fitting truth, perhaps the
only accuracy proclaimed in woe.

Bearing burdens consumed by need
for erudition, how distressing when
emptiness is the only revelation had.
Oh, heart of stone, my imploration
falls on ears of equal solidity but not
by choice; more so of preservation.
The shame is mine to own, in wealth
or pittance; a paltry line of subtlety.

This lament of grief, of devotion lost,
A heedless reverberation swallowed
up whole, then expelled in monotony.
Suffer not while smiles lie concealed
as stars under dark's asylum, an ideal
moment for obliviousness to overrule.
Now, immerse thyself in my position.
Do you hold me in the same regard?

Perhaps, distain stems from minute
chinks present in corroded armour;
imperfection begotten from wounds
tendered in war. An impulsive lapse.
Swept up in your fragrance, alluring
assault on my senses; an affirmation
of senselessness injected in transience.
To put aside fear, can this be done?

Conceding a meted taste of conjecture,
a rehearsal in adoration is warranted,
lest the ambush prospers without flaw.
What I seek is suspended by afflictions
strictly attuned to treachery, oh quaint.
Cunning heart, my death in your hands
is proper indeed, but still reserved for
emotions unattainable or apocryphal.

To shy away, a tragedy, for in depths
of eager souls are buried endless Edens.
Parting ways, at times, the only option
left to save what shred of love remains.
A prospect saturated with sadness grim.
For reckoning, I pray as summer spills
its final breath on currents vague with
indifference; so drifts the jaded heart.

Decisions

My mood, an unpredictable
tide crashing over me and I,
powerless to swim against it.
Instead, I give up and allow
the receding waters to take
me where they desire; it just
seems easier this way, less
expendable and exhausting.

To float along the plain that
separates us from reality and
inconsequential hypothesis;
It is necessary to differentiate
between the two, promptly.
To do otherwise may prove to
be disastrous to judgment.
But, it is no business of others.

I don't proclaim to harbour full
awareness of all that is strange
and distant in this world, but I
can safely say that I share a
kindred connection with the
ties that bind earth and heaven.
As I pass through the chaos of
my own mind, my choice is made.

Once the waves have crested,
there's no turning tail, even if it
was permitted, for passage is
granted once, and once only.
Life is a one way street and no
refunds are doled out to those
unsatisfied with the journey.
You shoulda read the fine print.

Fall From Favour

Master of trickery
slithers in stealth
to wrap thee in a
beguiling embrace.
Cocktail of poison;
foul and heinous
in design pollutes
the frail conscience.
Wandering deeper
into the dense forest,
circles of perplexity
are carved in soil;
Morals turn to dust.
A masterpiece in
progress to mould
as the artist wishes.
Each specimen a
unique canvass on
which the brush of
corruption applies
its distracting hues.
Prettiness leads us
astray, tarnishing
the real motive for
inflicting pain and
torment onto others.
By dragging down
our perceived rivals,
we in turn launch
ourselves onto an
impermanent and
unrealistic pedestal.
The descent is swift
and unsympathetic.

TRIBUTES

To the ones who gave us life....
To those who have passed....
To those who gave their lives....

A Mother's Love

A monarch unfurls her fiery wings
illuminated by the dawn's radiance.
Tiny droplets of sweetness adorn
emerald foliage in this new morn.
Pastel petals part, stretching up to
the rising sun, a bouquet so alluring.
These splendours are sweet in their
own special way, however; their
brilliance pales in her presence.

For nothing can compare to
the greatest beauty of all.
Her eyes are the sunshine,
her kiss, the gentle breeze
her voice, a lark's melody.

And her love....
Her love is

unconditional,
unwavering,
forever.

Daddy's Little Girl

It seems like only yesterday
that I was just a tiny child.
Your love for me never fails,
your scoldings, stern but mild.

It's strange to watch time fly
by so quickly before my eyes;
reminding me of the blessing
that we have you in our lives.

I have yet to feel another touch
that's as loving as your hand.
The closeness of our family
no one else will understand.

Each day the paths we walk
and journey on will change.
Reflections of your lasting
love in each of us remains.

You pointed out the righteous
path and led us along the way.
The wisdom you have planted,
we each still hold close today.

You sheltered us in childhood
and saw us through each day;
taught us of the Lord above,
About faith, and how to pray.

No matter where our lives may go,
we will trust the Lord above,
and through it all we'll thank him
for the gift of daddy's love.

Good-Bye Bluebird

How easily her face appears in
thought, even after all these years.
A sweet sight to behold indeed,
but peppered with melancholy;
like a rose forgotten by the sun.

Once, my Bluebird's song adorned
the ears like priceless diamonds;
a divine and melodious harmony.
Thawing the iciest and most callous
of souls; soothing the deepest sorrow.

Now, wings clipped by death, the
Bluebird sleeps - in peace, I pray.
Clad in eternal dusk, the world is
tersely denied the very epitome
of all that love and life denote.

In haste, I wash away my despair,
for somewhere in the confines
of my bruised heart, I do know
the Bluebird lives, and will eternally
spread her graceful wings for me.

As the coming dawn struggles
to escape the grasp of night,
I hear her voice once again;
maybe not expressed in speech,
but it is there nevertheless.

Locked away in the secret drawers
of my heart, my mind, my soul,
live my most cherished memories.
Here is where the Bluebird still soars
high, unchained, euphoric - immortal.

RIP Belinda....

I Wept

I wept,

For a child who aged too soon;
too young to know the truth.

I wept,

For those who perished at
the hands of budding youth.

I wept,

For eyes turned hard and black
that may never again see day.

I wept,

For you travelled down a path
and I can't follow you that way.

I wept,

For me, my own self lost.
Will I ever be the same?

I wept,

I weep, and always will,
and for that I feel no shame.

I know someday my heart will
heal and this child will return.

Life goes on; I've faced that fact,
but these memories I won't burn.

Ode to a Writer

Embedded deep inside my brain
an idea blooms from a tiny grain.

To arrange these thoughts
from madness to order is not
as easy as it may appear.

The only way to clear my head
is to allow my paper to be fed.

Through sleepless nights
new lives take form
and I their puppeteer.

The words that flow upon the page
whet thy appetite and set the stage.

At times I cry tears of joy
or mourn a fictitious loss
as if it were my own.

As I wind down my story's end,
despair at times my heart does rend.

And no matter the method
this narration plays out,
my mind and soul have grown.

In Gratitude of Silence

Silent now the soldiers sleep,
their tales long laid to rest.
I knew them not yet still I weep
and place a poppy o'er my breast.

Husbands, brothers, fathers, sons;
so brave and valiantly they fought.
Shores stained red, on hands and knees;
t'was our freedom that they sought.

Courageously they stood their ground
but freedom always carries a cost.
Thousands of men were wounded
and countless lives were lost.

So in gratitude of silence
and all of those who served,
sleep now, you have earned it.
Your peace is well deserved.

PART IV

For the Love of the Game

And so, the Sun departs this
aberrant world with quite a fuss;
pausing only to face the night
with one last show of defiance.
In vain, she flaunts a spectrum
of breathtaking hues and lustre.
Yet, despite this desperate front,
her role has come to fruition.
No imploration, prayer, nor appeal
can alter her imminent destiny.
I ponder this proud resistance;
this profound contempt that
the Sun harbours deep within.

Bullied by a more arcane and
cryptic rival, could her memory
be so brief and fleeting that she
fails to recall the day alone is hers?
The Moon cowers beyond the glare
of the Sun's final struggle for primacy.
Creatures of the night dare not show
their faces as their master slinks away.
This delay serves merely to promote
false hope and prolong the truth.
For the Moon will have his say.
Another link is added to the chain.

In truth, the act of Death holds but
one minute and trivial variation
from this timeless, unbroken dance.
'Tis true that once Life has turned
the final page in the book that has
been pre-written for each of us,
she is forced to stop her journey
for her trek has reached the end.
Less perplexing is her struggle
to remain than that of the Sun, for
this journey cannot be duplicated;
at least not in the same regard.

The Sun, the Moon; they engage
In a never-ending battle in which
neither party is destined to win.
Doomed are they in eternity to
repeat their predictable journey.
Ever so patient, Death waits her turn.
She may extend her visit in 'morn,
in dusk or by dawn's waning light.
Perhaps, even as the Sun takes her seat
in the highest pinnacle of the heavens.
Whenever Death enters into this party,
the rules are clear, and all must abide.

In the end – death always wins....

Rest Stop

I'm but a rest stop
for lonely drifters
as they search for
a place of anchor;
never meant to be
a final destination.

Just a brief detour
to use once before
washing away the
repulsive memory
of whatever time
was spent together.

The grey dissipates,
replaced with skies
of cerulean, which
leads me to await
your inevitable and
random appearance.

What can I not see?
Are my flaws really
so obvious that they
ooze unworthiness?
This abjection; I
won't lie, it stings.

For a time, I'm able
to lie to myself and
for a time, I believe
those beautiful lies.
But, time is fickle
and quite capricious.

I wonder if perhaps
I should seek out a
rest stop of my own
rather than investing
time and energy into
unrequited ambitions.

Tell Me No Lies

What is it exactly that
you feel you must hide?
What detestable secret
do you harbour inside?

Are you actions untrue
to those that you love?
Do you push others down
as you gloat from above?

These tales you weave
with convincing validity,
but once dissected apart,
are laced with stupidity.

What point does it prove,
this sanctimonious guile
you cover so plausibly
behind that mock smile?

Your life is constructed
by deception and spite.
I just can't comprehend
how you deem this is right.

Its witchery you cast on
your too-trusting friends.
Sit down, you dumb bitch,
I'll explain how this ends.

Webs are meant to entrap
prey, innocent and naive,
but what you don't know,
what you need to believe,

is the victim isn't always
the gullible or the meek,
at times its the asshole
Karma ruthlessly seeks.

She'll fuck up your mind;
you'll think you're the shit.
Then realize its too late, as
she kicks your ass in the pit.

You're stuck at rock bottom.
Oh my, how you'll suffer.
Doesn't matter to Karma,
for she'll just find another.

You'll be standing alone,
with no saviour; its true,
but just bear in mind, the
fault lies solely in you.

The Rose

I beheld a rose, once, beside a road;
its petals stretched out to the clear sky.
As I stood in awe of its perfect beauty,
a single question burned in my mind.

How could a treasure so precious yet frail
survive in such a cold, barren ground?
No lush, fertile soil enveloped its roots;
not a drop of water or food could be found.

Against unbalanced odds, this stunning rose
seemed to flourish without worry or care.
It wasn't until I truly opened my eyes,
I realized the answer had always been there.

All things in life, like this unyielding rose,
don't always spring up from the best.
Hard times and strife and sorrow and grief;
these tribulations put us all to the test.

Just when we think the burden's too harsh,
strength arises from deep in our soul.
Tenacity and spirit, a will to survive;
it all carries us to a common end goal.

Life is all about love; life is all about loss.
We will experience both pleasure and pain.
The key to survive – both body and mind,
is learning to smile through the heaviest rain.

Remember the rose if your heart ever hurts
and how it weathers the harshest conditions.
Strength and courage begin deep in the soul
With tenacity, you'll achieve your ambitions.

Truth or Dare

Jump in....

Do I dare?

The water's cold, and although
the thought of being numb and
apathetic is somewhat appealing,
I still can't bring myself to accept
the initial shock of the descent.
I guess I'll stay one step behind,
substituting sanity with shame,
basking in ignorance and neglect.

Remembering is a tedious chore
I'd prefer to consign to oblivion.

The knives have been withdrawn
and the stains have washed away,
but the scars and memories will
never evaporate, not while I still
hold a connection to this world.
If I close my eyes, I can almost
block out the bullshit; almost.

Its hard to tell where the line
between truth and lies is drawn.

I don't want to take the plunge
alone but I feel it's something
I must do without assistance.
The portal swings open but the
guest list is limited; by private
invitation only. I wonder if I'm
privy to such an exclusive gala.

Pity, I'm not dressed for the occasion.

Restless

The spirits are restless.
They cloud my thoughts
and pollute my dreams.
A jumble of curt voices
each clamouring to have
their sorrows heard first.
Oh, the vexations and
woes of the dead, how
they pique my attention.
These frivolous miseries;
misconceived notions to
those who continue to
walk among the living;
not realizing that they
are ghosts themselves.
Clarity, though droll and
absurd in nature, arrives
in abundance once the
realm of death is visible
and within hand's reach.
Regrets pour out like so
much foul and putrid pity.
It is our nature, as cursed
as it may sound, to turn a
blind eye to bleak affairs
of strife and awkwardness,
refusing to dwell on such
matters until so compelled.
Ignorance, at times, can
be a wonderfully blissful
attribute, even as it eats
away at our souls with
confounding jubilation.

Death's Sweet Lullaby

Now I lay me down to die.
Looking back, I won't ask why.

I've lost the will to take that step.
My actions make me feel inept.

What does it matter anyway?
When nothing changes day by day.

The same old shit, it clouds my mind.
I long to leave it all behind.

For what is love, if not returned?
Oh, countless times, my heart's been burned.

I close my eyes and wish for sleep.
I hope it's quick; I hope it's deep.

My life I leave in fate's cruel hand.
Memories fade like grains of sand.

As darkness comes to claim my soul,
I pray my sins you'll never know.

Institutionalized

Restrained from harm, but
not my disturbing thoughts.
Incarceration; an ineffective
solution to silence the voices
that chatter within my head.

Volume subdued; I acquire
a brief glimpse through the
parting curtain of lucidity.
Horrors; malevolent imps
merrily ridicule my sanity.

The haze, a wondrous and
heady feeling; it frees me.
From afar, rationale trips
an alarm; sensibility flees.
Relinquish complete control.

Tortured screams, how they
beg for release from pitiful
transgressions; clemency so
readily and cruelly denied.
They drip with familiarity.

Apprehension, it hangs in
the air with dread, disquiet.
Tucked away in isolation,
coldness seeps in unwanted,
a brutal rape of emotionality.

The door, it opens in protest.
An offer of deliverance; an
escape from this madness.
The scenery does not quite
live up to my expectations.

Unburdened by influences
both intimate and beyond,
the realization strikes me;
the asylum I long to elude
is my own damaged mind.

Keepers of the Dead

The agony....the agony
is instant and absolute.
An orgasmic crescendo;
intensity in its full glory.
awash in....abhorrence.

Ebbing tide, distant roar
of thunder, a brief echo
in another soul's world.
Only the wind can affirm
the remnants of my screams.

(Imaginary?) pressure
against my throat as
it is transformed into a
serrated abyss; here
flows a river of crimson.

How oddly comforting;
the spreading warmth
and the heavy dampness.
Blood....so much blood
pools between my breasts.

Vaguely, I struggle to
recall that final exhalation;
a subtle, feathery kiss, a
butterfly's sweet caress.
Soft, so soft and inviting.

Waning heat morphs into
frigidness. Cold...so cold.
It makes sense, (you'd think)
this compact cloak of finality.
I thought it would be warmer.

Figures, images, colours are
no longer astute – unfocused.
The connection with those
who still aimlessly roam the
domain of the living is lost.

Leaves beneath footsteps.
These leaves, my future;
kindred in time, eternal.
Devoid of spirit, vitality,
essence; devoid of....life.

Blackness and silence;
my new comrades for the
looming quest I must take.
I wait in my sarcophagus
of clay, soil, rocks, pebbles.

I hear them; it is imminent.
They come to devour me, to
pick away my sins, my worth.
The tenders of wayward bones,
the keepers of all that is dead.

I can't cry.
I can't beg.
I can't feel.
I can't move.
I can't scream.

I am dead.

Last Rites

'Tis a pity; your decision to cross my path,
for the sentence bequeathed is to feel my wrath.
Like a tiresome pest, your soul I'll smash

and curse you to the pits of hell.

Falsehood and trickery have left their stains.
Hypocrisy and deception will form your chains.
The sanity trickles from your rotting brain,

'til all that's left is an empty shell.

Time softens the sharpness of any pill.
My pain was inflicted of your own free will,
so vengeance is mine as your grave is filled;

unshackled from your crippling spell.

Revenge is a sweet, not bitter dish.
It's outcome greater than any wish.
Mouth and eyes now closed in stitch.

Deeply, I inhale your fading smell.

One last time, my back I'll turn.
I'll take with me a lesson learned.
Inside, I smile, for I know you'll burn.

On your expiration I refuse to dwell.

Arachnophobia

It creeps....closer,

its sluggishness,
methodical, decisive.
Each step a blade of
insanity driven deep
into the frail mind.

It stares....steadily,

through me, eyes
of evil, absolute.
Frozen; my gaze
weak, incapable of
retreat; adrift in fear.

It strikes....swift,

in its precision;
uncanny, expected.
Poison seeks refuge,
nestled inside me.
I rot from within.

It feeds....greedily,

how the intensity
explodes; I sense
the web of sanity
stretch, then snap.
My fate is sealed

R.I.P (Fuck that - Rot in Hell)

How does it feel
to be buried alive
with your sins?
Does it hurt
....much?

As the guilt
strips the flesh
from your bones
and burrows a nest
in your soul.

No longer a smile
adorning your face.
It is I who can laugh
as darkness is shed
from my heart.

Soon, even your
memory will fade,
to be hidden away
deep in the earth;
and no one will care.

Poison that spilled
from your lips
is stagnant now,
eternally wed to your
filth, to your stink.

Enjoy this hell,
built solely by lies
and promises killed.
I hope its cold and dark
where you sleep.

The Sands of Time

How procrastinating is time
for those who wallow in pain.
It dangles the rotting corpse of
optimism like a coveted prize.
The residual smugness is quite
enjoyable, so I would suspect.

The search is on for both truth
and closure, although it cannot
be ascertained if they are one
and the same, or merely ghosts
we relentlessly pursue in vain.
The reasons hold no validity.

Each thought, each idea, a tiny
granule of sand that sluggishly
pours through the murky glass.
How quickly they are forgotten
as they merge together; none
more remarkable than the rest.

For what is there to be found
once the final grain settles?
An empty silence, a pile of
loose dirt that, once turned
over simply begins the same
exact journey over once more.

An endless cycle of life and
death, sorrow and joy, pain
And pleasure; oh the cruelty!
The abrasions that scar your
Soul, how can they hold any
Worth? The clock winds down.

Tick tock....

Tick tock....

Tick tock....

ACROSTIC

All That Remains

A bewildering notion
Lingers in my mind. I
Long to reach out and

Take hold of the belief
Heaven in real and not
A fabricated rendering
That was created from

Radical embellishments.
Emerging from misled
Memories dashed with
A concoction of doubt,
I sense some truths are
Not meant to be divulged.
Still, hope hovers in wait.

Boston Bruins

Bashing rivals ruthlessly
On ice. Impossible to
Stop as they charge
The net. Striking fear in
Opponent's hearts with
Narcissistic precision.

Blood of black and gold
Runs through my veins.
Under my calm demeanour
Is a beast so passionate.
No one dare attempt to
Suppress my loyalty.

Emotional Clarity

Effectively exuding a
Mixture of emotions,
Our hearts are ever
Twisting in turmoil.
Is it not perplexing;
Our demented, askew
Notion of love? Rather
Apathetic illusion -
Love as an emotional

Charge between two
Like souls, fused in fate.
A more likely cause of
Reverent adoration?
Its just carnal confusion
That we feel. Don't allow
Your heart to be deceived.

Everything in its Place

Obtuse are the
Beliefs of the
Sane and wise.
Each of us holds
Sanity by a mere
String, weak and
Infirm in nature.
Vexing to me, the
Enigma we hold. A

Complex doctrine
Of perfect order
Manifesting from
Perfect anarchy.
Undaunted, we
Lie to ourselves.
Shall I explain?
In my world, I
View precision in
Every aspect. I

Don't expect to
Instil my quirks
Selfishly into
Others, but I do
Rest in ease once
Discord is gone.
Each thing must
Remain in place.

Ghosts of the Past

Guided by melancholy.
Haunted by mementos
Of fleeting snapshots
Scattered haphazardly.
Teasing unmercifully,
Sending our last shreds

Of sanity to yonder realms
Fraught with nostalgia.

Tasty morsels of hope
Hollow out our souls.
Every exhaled breath

Propels foolish fallacies.
As memories fade, they
Speak woeful whispers of
Times never to return.

Insomnia

A whirlwind of jumbled thoughts
Not patterned in any semblance
Or order, just....random, arbitrary.
The clock ticks; seconds, minutes,
Hours creep by with deliberate sloth.
Enjoying my suffering, the moon
Rests, quiet amber amid ebony ink.

Sleep scurries into hiding; a secret
Lair devoid of dreams. There, it
Eagerly observes me with vacant
Eyes, leaving me once again to
Ponder unsolvable riddles that
Loiter in the crevasses of my
Endlessly inquisitive mind.
Softly, I offer an imploration for
Slumber to sacrifice me to the

Night; consume my cognizance.
Instead, sleep plays its relentless
Games, while I wonder if I'll ever
Have the chance to dream again.
The dawn breaks; I am exhausted.

Inspire Me

Its been said that
Nothing in this life
Seems fair or just.
Pathetic, the inane
Idea to smile as it
Rains and hoping
After a storm that
The rainbow will
Instil motivation
Or grant strength.
Nothing irks more.

Change is inevitable;
Obligations breed
Madness; from our
Errors we learn to
Succeed. Frump and

Folly with a side of
Ridiculousness. We
Offer alleviation with
Meaningless drivel.

Words that echo with
Insipidness. Firmly
Tangled up, are we,
Holding onto adages
Instead of pursuing
Notions of our design.

Make Me a Believer

Morning sweeps in swift
As the night absconds with
Kindred spirits in her wake.
Eluding sleep, instead I await

Myriads of vagary that fail to
Emerge. Yes, I still hold faith in

An ethereal, parallel existence.

Belief is a powerful drug we
Each devour with eagerness,
Letting it cloud our minds with
Idiosyncrasies of peculiarity.
Even as truth explodes with
Vividness beyond reality, I
Envision transversing worlds,
Realizing that I do believe.

Obscured By Shadows

Obsidian figures in my wake
Betrothed without concession.
Show yourself to me instead of
Cowering like a filthy mongrel
Under the cover of darkness.
Reluctance solidifies belief in
Existence of secrets not to be
Divulged, though I am worthy.

Bask in the power you hold on
Yonder souls in search, for it

Shall be fleeting at best, I'm sure.
Have you no shame, or is this
Ability to create such a complex
Debacle come as a natural talent?
Once light exposes the verity of
What you really entail, then so
Shall transgressions be redeemed.

Ode to Karma

Karma, my sweet....
As sure as the
Rains absolve
My own sins, I
Am with faith.

Your justice, with-
Out mercy, swift.
Under aloof and

Wary eye, a curse
On man's hypocrisy.
No being on earth
Dare boast to be
Exempt from thy
Reckoning or wrath.
For to scoff at such fate -
Undeniably, without
Lasting concern, a

Bane on his soul.
In all poor, wretched
Truth, such recourse
Carries retribution.
Her justice be served.

Reflections

Rarely is my judgement considered sound or coherent.
Evidently, I'm not wise in the ways of recognizing the
Faults and flaws that others carry around in pretence.
Likewise, I lack the ability to perceive my own defects,
Enervations, and frailties. You see, when I glance at the
Contemplative vision that silently returns my stare, the
Truth cannot be concealed. No matter how alluring the
Image appears, no amount of primping or polishing can
Offer solace from the tribulations that lay beneath the
Neatly attired disguise. I pick at my own flaws, a
Scavenger of reclusive souls; eradicator of decency.

Instilled into our minds, we hold on to the narcissistic
Notion that we retain complete control over every

Complexity and entanglement that extends from the ir-
Rational and the absurd. The restrictions we place on
Authorityawait excision from our personalities; putrid
Cancerous growths that metastasize and eventually
Kill any hope or aspiration that lingers within our
Egotistic selves. A cumbersome trek, one that we
Delve into with such unimpeded relish and impulsivity.

Gossamer webs disperse threadlike fingers in scattered
Layers of duplicity. Such blatant intricacy ensures that
Any unsavoury attributes are benevolently overlooked.
Systematically, we are oblivious to the commitment of
Senseless acts; our true self is put on exhibit for all.

Suicide Solutions

Solitude is a soul mate mis-
Understood by those whose
Inner demons have stealthily
Conned them into believing
Its somehow abnormal to
Delve into one's own psyche.
Eventually, the essence of the

Soul is diminished because
Of despotic, oppressive axioms.
Lesions of despondency bloom
Underneath the brave exterior,
Taxing vivacity and aspirations.
Instead, the voices of dysphoria
Offer encouraging words of
Negativity. Being dead inside
Sells the solution effortlessly.

My original plan was to add a glossary for some of the unusual terms and phrases I used in many of the preceding poems. After tossing this idea around for some time, I decided against it. Some things are better left to one's own imagination or interpretation. However, if you lay sleepless at night, agonizing over the divine purpose of my words and curiosity wins out; feel free to google the meanings. Who knows, you may learn something new, and perhaps, even gain a tiny piece of insight into what makes my warped mind tick....

About the Author

Debbie Holick lives in Medicine Hat, Alberta, Canada. She is the mother of two beautiful daughters – Brooklyn (The Aspiring Artist) and Arianna (The Sports Nut). They live quiet lives, occasionally interrupted in the wee hours of the morning by their cats, Chip AKA 'Crack Cat', and Pixie.

Debbie began writing at an early age, accumulating countless journals of random thoughts and ideas that eventually do blend together to create sometimes heartbreaking, sometimes funny, and sometimes morbid tales. Most of her ideas stem from personal experiences, worldly observations and vivid dreams.

Her first novel Playing With Fire, was published in 2010. She also published a book of poetry Dreamstate, under the name Debbie Wilk. Look for several novels to be available over the next few years.

Remember to always follow your dreams and never let anyone tell you that you can't. They are fucking liars....

Excerpt from:

The Final Awakening
By

Debbie Holick

Available Spring 2015

Decisions, Decisions - Part 1....

We all have choices to make. After all, isn't that what life is about; making choices? When the alarm clock goes off at the crack of dawn every morning, we choose to either jump out of bed or bitchslap it into stunned silence before choosing to do it all over again in another 10 minutes. We choose our career path, who we will marry, whether or not to pay the monthly bills or spend our last few dollars on a case of beer for the weekend; we choose to shit or get off the pot, as my father used to say. You get the idea.

Yes, we all have choices to make in our lives. But, I thought being a child wouldn't mean having to make such complex decisions. I thought it meant choosing which stuffed animal to sleep with at night, which colour of ribbon to put in my hair; I thought it meant picking Captain Crunch over Frosted Flakes in my groggy morning stupor.

I was a child, but in many ways I had gained wisdom far beyond my years here on earth; far more wisdom than you will probably ever gain in your own lifetime. I didn't want to make this decision. I am still a child and it shouldn't be up to me to choose. This particular verdict should only be reserved for a higher power. Not me.....not me.

Yet, here I was; glancing between the two books that Destiny had offered up to me. One I recognized but the other was foreign to me and it reminded me of the time my mother had taken me to The Cherry Blossom Restaurant the first time I tried sushi. When the beautiful, yet seemingly mute, Japanese woman placed the plate in front of me, I unconsciously wrinkled my nose at the sight of the tiny parcels of rice, seaweed and fish tucked neatly inside. It was inviting yet revolting at the same time.

That same feeling inched its way into my gut as my gaze alternated between the two books. They had appeared out of nowhere; an amateurish magician's trick without the smoke and mirrors, sitting side by side on an intricately carved table that reeked of ancient secrets and mysteries.

I reached my hand out and stroked the cover of the book to my left, slowly as if I wanted to absorb every detail of its slightly rough covering. The spine was slightly worn, as you could expect on any well read book. The owner must have loved the stories buried inside so much as to risk its potential destruction.

My attention turned to the second book, which appeared brand new and unopened. The cover felt gritty under my clammy palm and as I swiped my hand over top, I uttered a quick cough to clear my throat of the dust and dirt I had disturbed.

My frown quickly turned to an expression of wariness and understanding as my eyes flew back to the first book. The claws of fear had a stranglehold on my insides.

"Maddy."

That one word was spoken so softly and without any emotion, yet it held so much meaning. I knew I was delaying the inevitable. I was killing time before making the decision that would likely alter the course of my life forever.

I knew what she wanted me to do. It was so obvious a simple child could have come to that conclusion. I laughed bitterly to myself. A child. Oh, the irony. I had learned many things of late; the definition of irony being one of them. If only my teacher could see me now. I smiled again, but her voice, her fucking voice wiped it off my face in an instant. Impatience oozed out like a stinking, green pus.

"Maddy."

I turned around, determined to put this off as long as possible. Perhaps if I stretched it out long enough, I could make the books disappear. After all, they had appeared out of nowhere; they could go back where they came from just as quickly. Then I wouldn't have to choose. It was a cowardly tactic, but never once have I proclaimed to be a hero or a leader.

"I can't do this. I just can't."

"You have to Maddy. You know you have to."

"But why?" I could hear the whininess weaving itself throughout each word and I hated myself for it.

"Every movement you've made, every word, every action....they've all led you here Maddy. It was you who picked the path you walked along. No one but you."

"But that's not true." I protested.

"Maddy." Her voice was soothing now, like a gentle wave lapping on a sandy shore. "You know the truth."

And the reality of it was, I really did know the truth. I had known it all along. It had just taken me until this very moment to accept it. Truth didn't come to me as an epiphany, slamming into my consciousness like a tsunami. It didn't creep up slowly like a lioness stalking her prey. No. The truth was just....there. It had been there all along, I had just chosen to ignore it. Another choice a child shouldn't have had to make....I thought bitterly.

Suddenly, it dawned on me what the actual decision was that I was about to make. I spun around once more, but this time my voice wasn't laced with fear or uncertainty; only contempt. It was at this moment that I was no longer a child. She could sense it too. Each word it home, like daggers piercing the heart of a wicked beast.

"I do know the truth. I know what I must do."

She nodded in confirmation.

Against my will, I did her bidding. There was really no question. I'm not sure if I did it out of spite, or because a part of me was terrified to tempt fate or if it was just pure, childish curiosity. Regardless, I did it.

My hand reached out to the left book; the one I had first laid eyes on when they had both appeared. It seemed only logical to open this one first. I would open this one, and then the other, like a child dutifully obeying her mother.

I closed my eyes briefly, trying to stop the tears that were welling up inside. I could feel them burning under my eyelids. In spite of my efforts, one managed to squeeze its way past my thick lashes and dribble down my cheek.

I could see the image of my mother in the darkness. I hadn't thought of my mother in a long time. I hoped she missed me a much as I missed her.

I inhaled deeply, knowing I could hesitate no longer. No more delays. No more second thoughts about what I was about to do. The only thoughts that fluttered through my mind in those few brief seconds were of the events leading up to this one, last decision....